# The WORD of GOD Will Take ACTION

CHARITY TURNER

Copyright © 2019 by Charity Turner

All rights reserved.

No part of this book may be reproduced, distributed or transmitted in any form, by any means, graphic, electronic, or mechanical, including photocopy, recording, taping, or by any information storage or retrieval system, without permission in writing from the publisher, except in the case of reprints in the context of reviews, quotes, or references.

Unless otherwise indicated, all scriptures are taken from the Holy Bible, King James Version, which is in the public domain.

Published by:
Claire Aldin Publications
P.O. Box 453
Southfield, MI 48037

Library of Congress Control Number: 2019912832

ISBN: 978-1-7336560-4-7
Printed in the United States of America.

For this is good and acceptable in the sight of God Our Savior; who will have all men to be saved, and to come unto the knowledge of the truth.

~1 Timothy 2:3-4 KJV

# DEDICATION

May our Lord bless us all as we live, preach, teach and write. Fulfilling His great commission to ready a people with wisdom and righteousness for the coming of the Lord is the goal.

# TABLE OF CONTENTS

Prologue ................................................. 11

A Note from the Author ....................... 13

Section 1: Praying the Word of God ... 15

Section 2: Praying in Jesus' Name ...... 56

Section 3: Praying Specific Concerns .. 92

About the Author ................................. 107

# PROLOGUE

God is the judge. He alone decides who wins and who loses, not your opponent. God said we are going to win. It does not matter what it looked like when you went down. He said, "I'm telling you to hold on to your faith because you are surely coming out!"

# A NOTE FROM THE AUTHOR

I had a dream that I was at my childhood home, and I had a pet snake. A relative and I was in the living room, and he said to me "Put the snake up to your face and let it kiss you". I said "No! It may bite me". He then put the snake up to his face and it did not bite him, but I still didn't do it. We then went out on the porch. I asked him not to put the snake down because it might run away. He said, "It won't run away…it's your pet". He put it down anyway, and as soon as he did, the snake ran so fast across the street that I blinked my eyes and it was gone.

Three months before I had this dream I started praying this prayer:
*Father, how can I know all the sins lurking in my heart? Cleanse me, Father God, from these hidden faults. Keep me from deliberate sins, and don't let them control me. Then I will be free of guilt and innocent of great sin. I ask that the words of my mouth, and the thoughts of my heart be pleasing to*

*you Father because You are my Rock and Redeemer, in Jesus Name. Amen.*

~Based on Psalms 19:12-14

You see, faith comes by hearing and hearing by the Word of God (Romans 10:17). God has given us authority to speak a thing and it be established in our lives. The Word of God is like a seed. We must meditate on that Word day and night until it takes root in our spirit or becomes real to us. It then builds up our faith, and we have the confidence to walk in what we prayed.

My name is Evangelist Charity Turner. I am a born again child of the Living God. God has delivered me from the pits of hell, so to speak. I received Jesus into my heart and I have been engrafted into God's royal family. He sat me down to teach me, then lifted me up, and gave me the authority to speak a thing and it be established. My God has blessed me to write prayers from His Word. The Word of God is action and it has power. I believe when a person reads these prayers, the anointing of the Word of God will take action in their lives.

# SECTION 1: PRAYING THE WORD OF GOD

Let me draw near to You, Father God, with a sincere heart in full assurance of my faith, having my heart sprinkled and cleansed from a guilty conscience, and having my body washed with pure water. Let me hold on unwaveringly to the hope that I profess, for my God has promised and He is faithful. Let me consider how I may encourage others to have love and to do good deeds. Let us not give up coming together, as some are in the habit of doing, but let us encourage one another as we see the Day of the Lord approaching.

~Based upon Hebrews 10:22-25

I know that some of the people whom I love intended to harm me, but You, Father God, intended it for my good. To accomplish what is now being done by the saving of many lives, God will bless me to provide for the ones I love and their children.

~Based on Genesis 50:20-21

Worthy is the Lamb of God that was slain so that I may receive power, riches, wisdom, strength, honor, glory and blessings. The blessings will cause me to have favor, and I'll get anything I request according to His Word. God will turn things around for me in just days.

~Based on Revelation 5:11-12

I will always remember Father God. It is You who gives me the power to become rich. You do it to fulfill the covenant You made with my forefathers.

~Based on Deuteronomy 8:18

Danger is real, but fear is a choice. God has not given us the spirit of fear but power, love, and a sound mind. I thank You, Father, for not giving me the spirit of fear.

~Based on 2 Timothy 1:7

Father, I ask you to raise me up for Yourself to be faithful in the work you have given me. I will do according to what is in Your heart, and in Your mind. Thank you for building me a sure house so I will walk among Your anointed forever.

~Based on 1 Samuel 2:35

It is a good thing to give thanks unto the Lord, and to sing praises unto His name. Although the wicked flourish like weeds, and evildoers blossom with success, there is only eternal destruction ahead of them. The godly will flourish like palm trees and grow strong for we are planted in the house of the Lord. We will still bear fruit in our old age, remaining vital and fresh to declare that the Lord is our rock. He is just and there is nothing but goodness in Him.

~Based on Psalms 92:1-7; 12-15

When I am suffering and in pain, I ask God to rescue me by His saving power. Then I will praise God with singing and honor Him with thanksgiving, for this will please God. By being humble, I will see my God at work in my life and be glad. Let all who seek God's help live in joy. For the Lord hears the cries of His people, and He does not despise His people who are oppressed. For God will save His people and lift them up. They will take possession of the land, and those who love Him will live there in safety.

~Based on Psalms 69:29-36

I will worship You, Father, in Your sanctuary, and come into Your presence. Help me to lead a blameless life, and do what is right, speaking the truth with a sincere heart. Help me not to slander others, or harm neighbors or friends. I pray for the people who know they are sinning, but keep doing it, and I honor the people who follow the Lord. I keep my promises even when it hurts, and lend money without interest. I don't accept bribes against the innocent. I am thankful to stand firm forever before You.

~Based on Psalms 15: 1-5

I confess with my mouth that Jesus Is Lord, and I believe in my heart that God raised Him from the dead, and I am now saved. With my heart, I believe unto righteousness, and with my mouth my confession is made unto salvation.

~Based on Romans 10:9-10

My heart is confident in You, O God. No wonder I can sing Your praises, even with my soul!

~Based on Psalms 108:1

I am a king, and I believe that when I give a command, it will be carried out. It is the same with my word; I send it out, and it always produces my desire. It will accomplish all I want it to, and it will prosper everywhere I send it.

~Based on Isaiah 55:11

Our Father who is in heaven, hallowed be thy name. Thy kingdom come. Thy will be done, in earth as it is in heaven. I ask that You bless me, and enlarge my territory. Let Your hand be with me, and keep me from harm so that I am free from trouble and pain.

~Based on 1 Chronicles 4:10

I thank You, Father, that Your word is a lamp to my feet and a light to my path.

~Based on Psalms 119:105

Father, I ask that You give me the ability to have great wisdom, to render decisions with justice.

~Based on 1 Kings 3:28

As I cast forth my bread upon the water, any day now, I will see my loaves of bread. I will trade my goods with other nations and get a return. During my journey, I will encounter winds and storms, for I know not what evil may come, but I will battle through. Once I've done the trade, I will be laden with valuables. This is an investment that will come to me in troubled times, so I don't withhold giving gifts or resources for others. I am faithful and steadfast in my daily life. Bad things happen. We can't change people; all we can do is control our response to them. Despite the evil and unexpected things, we must keep busy in the Lord.

~Based on Ecclesiastes 11:1

God said, He created me, He formed me, He has called me by my name, and I am His. He told me that when I go through deep waters and great trouble, He will be with me; He will be with me when I go through rivers of difficulty. He will not let me down. Even when I walk through the fire of oppression, I will not be burned; the flames will not consume me because He is the Lord my God, the Holy One of Israel, my Savior.

~Based on Isaiah 43:1-3

Therefore, since I have been made right in God's sight by faith, I have peace with God because of what my Lord Jesus Christ did for me. I have also gained access by faith. Grace, in which I now stand, is the place of the highest privilege, joyfully looking forward to sharing God's Glory.

~Based on Romans 5:1-2

☐

I tell myself with to praise the Lord my whole heart and for me to never forget the good things He does for me. He forgives all my sins, and heals my diseases. He ransomed me from death, and surrounds me with His love. He fills my life with good things, and my youth is renewed like the eagles. He gives me righteousness and justice, and makes sure I'm treated fairly. He reveals to me His character and deeds. He is merciful, and gracious, and slow to anger. I know because He has not punished me for sins, as I deserve. His unfailing love toward me, because I love Him, is great. The rebellious acts I had are far from me. God is my Father, I am His child, and I love Him. His salvation will extend to my children's children because I will teach them to be faithful of His commands, laws, and decrees. My God has made heaven His throne, where He rules over everything. I will serve him and do His will all my life.

~Based on Psalms 103

When trouble comes my way, my faith is tested, and I have a chance to grow. When the endurance of my faith is fully developed, I am then mature and complete in the Lord, lacking nothing.

~Based on James 1:1-4

May the Lord bless me, and protect me. May the Lord smile on me, and be gracious to me. May the Lord turn His face to me, show me His favor and give me peace.

~Based on Numbers 6:24-26

Oh, how my soul praises the Lord, and my spirit rejoices in God my Savior. For He took notice of the humble state of His child, and now generation after generation will call me blessed. For He has done great things for me.

His mercy goes to those who love Him. He has performed mighty deeds with His arms. He scatters those who are proud in their innermost thoughts. He has taken down rulers from their thrones, but exalted the humble. He has filled the hungry with good things, and sent away the rich with empty hands. He has helped His children, and He has not forgotten His promise to be merciful, even as He said to our forefathers.

~Based on Luke 1:47-55

O Lord, my God, how great You are! You are robed in honor, and dressed in a robe of light. You make clouds your chariots; the winds are Your messengers. You placed the world on its foundation so it would never be moved. You sent rain on the mountains from Your heavenly home, and You filled the earth with the fruit of Your labor. You caused plants to grow for us to use, and produced food, wine, olive oil as lotion for our skin, and bread to give us strength. You made the moon to make the seasons, and the sun that knows when to set. You sent the darkness, and it became night. What a variety of things You made with Your wisdom. We depended on You, Lord, to give us food. You opened Your hand, and we were satisfied. But when You hid Your face and turned from us, we panicked, as if You took our breath from us, and we then died and turned to dust. Afterwards, You sent Your Spirit and new life was born, and You renewed our face on the earth. May Your glory last forever, and I will praise You with my last breath.

~Based on Psalms 104

I seek first the Kingdom of God, and His righteousness, and all things will be added unto me.

~Based on Matthew 6:33

I ask that You hear my prayer O Lord, let my cry come to You. Do not hide Your face from me in my day of trouble. Incline Your ear to me in the day that I call and answer me speedily, Father.

~Based on Psalms 102:1,2

I thank You, Father God, that I am not conformed to this world, but I am transformed by the renewing of my mind that I may prove what is the good, acceptable and perfect will of God through me.

~Based on Romans 12:2

Revelation brings me to a place of believing and what I believe is what God will give me and what I will become for as I thinketh in my heart, so am I.

~Based on Proverbs 23:7

Lord, have mercy on Your people. See how we suffer at the hand of those who hate us? Snatch us back from the jaws of death. Save us so we can praise You publicly in this world, so we can rejoice that You have rescued us. The nations have fallen into the pit they dug for others. They have been caught in their own trap. You, Lord, are known for our justice. The wicked have trapped themselves in their own snares. The wicked will go down to the grave, and this is the fate of all nations who ignore God! For the needy will not be forgotten forever; the hopes of the poor will not be crushed. Arise, O Lord! Let the nations be judged in Your presence! Make them tremble in fear, O Lord. Let them be caught in the evil they plan for others. Let them know they are only merely human. Father, save us from the clutches of the powerful, so that at last we have hope, and the fangs of the wicked are broken against us.

~Based on Psalms 9:13-20

I looked for a man among you who might rebuild the wall of righteousness, that guards the land, to stand in the gap before Me, on behalf of the land, so I wouldn't have to destroy it, but I found no one.

~Based on Ezekiel 22:30

I will fulfill the vows I made to You, O Lord, the vows I made to You when I was deep in sin. That is why I sacrifice myself to You with my tithes and offerings. I will tell the whole world what You have done for me. I cried out to you, God, for help and if I had not confessed my sins in my heart, You would not have listened to me. But God, You did listen. You paid attention to my prayer. All praise be to You, who have not rejected my prayer or withheld His unfailing love from me.

~Based on Psalms 66:13-20

Let the redeemed of the Lord speak out to tell others that He redeemed us from our enemies. He has gathered us from many lands - some from the wilderness, the wastelands, the desert, finding nowhere to settle the lost and homeless, the hungry and thirsty, those nearly dead. Then we cried out to the Lord in our troubles and He delivered us from our distress. He led us to go straight, and we were safe in a city of habitation we were settled, and we can live. We thank You, and praise You, Lord, for Your unfailing love and wonderful deeds, for You filled the hungry with good things and quenched our thirst.

~Based on Psalms 107:2-9

I pray that God, the Father of my Lord and Savior Jesus Christ, also the Father of Glory, grant to me the spirit of wisdom and revelation, which will give me deep, personal and intimate insight into the knowledge of Him.

~Based on Ephesians 1:17

I am the righteousness of God, as bold as a lion, in which I am strongest among others. I will not turn away from any one in speaking the truth of the Gospel of Jesus.

~Based on Proverbs 28:1-30:30

O God, whom I praise, do not stand silent, for deceitful men have opened their mouths and are telling lies about me. They are all around me with their hateful words spoken against me. They fight and attack me without cause. I love them, but they try to destroy me, even as I am praying for them. They repay me evil for my good, and hatred for my love. Father, I ask that You bring them to trial, judge them, let them be found guilty, and may their prayers condemn them. May another take their leadership. May the creditor seize all they have. May no one take pity or extend kindness to them. May their family name be blotted out in a single generation. May their sins always remain before You, Lord, for they have refused to give thought of doing kindness to others, and persecute the poor and needy. Cursing is as much a part of them as their clothing. Now may their curse return to them like a belt, and be tied around them forever. May this be the Lord's punishment to them who are plotting against my life.

~Based on Psalms 109:1-20

Thanks be to God, which always causeth me to triumph in Christ, and wherever I go, God uses me to tell others about Jesus. The good news of the knowledge of Him is like a sweet smelling perfume in every place.

~Based on 2 Corinthians 2:14

I will Praise You, O Lord, because I am happy. I delight in doing Your commands. My children are blessed and successful. Wealth and riches are in my house, and my righteousness will endure forever. Even when darkness overtakes me, my light will come bursting through, and show that I am still gracious, compassionate, and a righteous person. All goes well for me because I am gracious. I conduct my business affairs fairly, so evil will not overcome me, and people will remember me. I have no fear of bad news because my heart is steadfast in trusting in You, Lord. I am confident, and fearless knowing that I can face my enemies and triumph. I give to the poor and needy, and my good deeds will not be forgotten…they are honored. The wicked will see me, and be grieved. He will gnash his teeth in anger; his longing to be like me will come to nothing.

~Based on Psalms 112

Not to us, O Lord, but to Your name be the glory because of Your love and faithfulness. Why do nations say "Where is their God?" Our God is in heaven, and He does whatever pleases Him, but the other nation's idols are silver and gold made by the hands of men. They have mouths that cannot speak, eyes that cannot see, ears that cannot hear, noses that cannot smell, hands that cannot feel, feet that cannot walk, nor can they speak through their throat. Those who make the idols are just like them and so is every one who trusts in them.

~Based on Psalms 115:1-8

I thank You, Father God, that Your divine power gives me everything I need for living a godly life. You have called me to receive Your own glory, and goodness. By that same mighty power, You have given me all Your riches and wonderful promises. You have promised that I will escape the corruption all around me in this world caused by evil desires.

~Based on 2 Peter 1:3-4

I thank You, Father God, that I am one of Your children whose rebellion is forgiven and whose sin is put out of Your sight! When I refused to confess my sin, I was weak and miserable, and I groaned all day long. Day and night, Your hand of discipline was heavy on me. My strength evaporated like water in the summer heat. Finally, I confessed all my sins to You, Lord, and I stopped trying to hide them. You forgave me of all my sins, and all my guilt went away. I pray that all people confess their sins to You, Lord, while there is still time. Then the Lord said, "I will guide you along the best pathway for your life. I will advise you, and watch over you. Don't be like senseless people who need to be bribed to keep them under control. Many sorrows come to the wicked, but unfailing love surrounds those who trust the Lord. So rejoice in the Lord, and be glad. Shout for joy, all whose hearts are pure".

~Based on Psalms 32

With God's help, I will do mighty things, for He will trample down my enemies. Father, let me live forever in Your sanctuary, safe beneath the shelter of Your wings. Father, You have an inheritance reserved for me because I respectfully fear Your name. I ask that You add many years to my life, and may my years span for generations, and may I reign under Your protection forever. Appoint Your unfailing love and faithfulness to watch over me. I wait quietly before You, Father, because

my hope is in You. You alone are my rock, my salvation, and my fortress, where I know I will not be shaken. When my wealth increases, I will not make it the center of my life. My salvation and my honor comes from you along, Father God, because You are my refuge, a rock where no enemy can reach me.
~Based on Psalms 60:12-61:4-7-62:5-7, 10


Now that I am old and gray, do not abandon me, O God. I will praise You more and more. I will tell every one about Your righteousness all day long. I proclaim Your saving power. I praise Your mighty deeds, O God. I will tell everyone You are just and good. Let me proclaim Your power to this new generation, and tell about Your mighty miracles to all who come after me. You have done such wonderful things. Who can compare with You, O God? I have suffered much hardship, but You restored me to life again, and You restored me to an even greater honor and comfort than I once was. That is why I praise

You with music and songs, because You are faithful to Your promises, O God.
~Based on Ephesians 6:10,11

I will never be sick or broke another day in my life because You, Father, said in Your Word that You will increase me more, and more, and more.
~Based on Psalms 115:14

I believe that it is a good thing to give thanks unto the Lord, and to sing praises unto His name. Although the wicked flourish like weeds, and evildoers blossom with success, there is only eternal destruction ahead of them. The godly will flourish like palm trees and grow strong, for we are planted in the house of the Lord. I will still bear fruit in my old age, and remain vital and fresh. I will declare that the Lord, is my rock; He is just, and there is nothing but goodness in Him.
~Based on Psalms 92:1,7, 12-15

I will bless You, Lord God, O God of Israel. You alone do such wonderful things. I ask

that You use me to rescue the poor when they cry for help and the oppressed who have no one to defend them. Give justice to me, O God. Help me to judge Your people righteously and in the right way. Allow me to defend the poor, to rescue the children of the needy, and to crush their oppressors. Let the poor always be treated fairly. I ask that there be abundant prosperity for all until the end of time. I ask that my enemies fall before me in the dust, because I know that my life is precious to You, Lord, and I praise Your glorious name forever.
~Based on Psalms 72:1-19

Father, I will sing of Your love and justice and I will Praise you with songs. Father, I will be careful to live a blameless life, and I will walk with integrity. With You, Father, I will set no wicked thing before my eyes, and I will have nothing to do with the crooked dealings, and I will reject evil. I will not tolerate conceit or pride or put up with people that slander others. My eyes shall be upon the faithful, and He who walks blameless will minister to me, not anyone that is deceitful or tell lies. Every morning, I will pray that the evildoers be destroyed and cut off.

~Based on Psalms 101

And this is the confidence and belief that I have in God. That if I ask anything according to His will, He hears me, and if I know that God, hears whatever I ask, I know that I have the request that I desired from Him.

~Based on 1 John 5:14, 15

I am not afraid of anything. I will just stand where I am and watch the Lord rescue me. The inhabitant that I see today will never be seen again. The Lord will fight for me, and I won't have to lift a finger in my defense!

~Based on Exodus 14:13

Father, I ask You to fill me with Your spiritual discernment, sound knowledge, and Your will through all spiritual wisdom and understanding. Then, the way that I live will always honor and please You, Lord. I will continually do good and kind things for others. All the while, I will learn to know You better and better. I pray that You strengthen me with Your glorious power so that I will have all the patience and endurance I need. Fill me with Your joy, and I thank You for enabling me to share the inheritance that belongs to Your holy people who live in the light.

~Based on Colossians 1: 9-11

Father, how can a young person keep their ways pure? Is it by obeying Your ways and following Your word? I have tried my best to find You; I seek You with all my heart. Father, do not let me stray from Your commands. I have hidden Your word in my heart that I might not sin against You. Praise be to You, O Lord, to teach me Your decrees. With my lips, I have recited out loud all the law You have given me. I rejoice in following Your decrees as one rejoice in riches. I study Your commands, and I have respect for Your ways. I will delight myself in Your statutes, and I will not forget Your word.

~Based on Psalms 119: 9-16

Be anxious for nothing, but in everything by prayer and supplication, with Thanksgiving. I let my requests be made known to God, and the peace of God, which surpasses all understanding, will guard my heart, and mind through Christ Jesus. To make a humble request, to go beyond the limit, ask, pray, believe and receive. I expect to receive when I ask God for anything.

~Based on Philippians 4: 6-7


Deal bountifully with me, Lord, Your servant, so that I may live, and keep Your Word. Open my eyes that I may see the wonderful things in Your law; do not hide Your commands from me. My soul longs for Your laws at all times. I know that You will rebuke the arrogant who are cursed, and those who stray from Your word. I ask that You remove from me reproach, and contempt because I obey Your principles. Even though leaders sit and slander me, I, Your servant continue to meditate on Your word. I delight in Your statutes because they counsel me, and give me wise advice.

~Based on Psalms 119:17-24

The Spirit of the Lord speaks through me, His words are upon my tongue. Father God has made a covenant with me that is eternal, final, and sealed. He will constantly look after my safety and success, and I will be a leader over men in righteousness, because I do fear the Lord My God.

~Based on 2 Samuel 23: 1-2, 5

Father, O how I love Your law! I think on it all day long. Your commands are my constant guide which makes me wiser than my elders, wiser than my enemies, and I have more insight than my teachers. I have kept my feet from every evil path, so that I may remain obedient to Your word. I have not turned away from Your laws, for You have taught me well. I gain understanding from Your word; it's a wonder I hate every false, and wrong way of life. Your word is a lamp to my feet, and a light for my path. I have sworn and will perform Your righteous laws. I have suffered much, O Lord, and You have restored my life again, as You promised. Lord, accept my grateful praise of thanks, and I ask that You teach me more about Your laws for I am determined to keep Your principles to the end.

~Based on Psalms 119: 97-112

I lift up my eyes to You, O Lord, to You whose throne is in heaven. I look to You, O Lord, my God, for Your mercy. Just as a maid would look to the hand of her mistress, so shall my eyes look to the Lord my God. Show me Your mercy. Have mercy on me, O Lord God Almighty. Have mercy on me, for I have had my fill of contempt. Save me from this cruel, proud and arrogant world.

~Based on Psalms 123

Restore our fortunes, O Lord, as streams renew in the desert. Those who sow with tears will reap a harvest with songs of joy. He who goes out weeping, carrying seed to sow, will return with songs of joy carrying his harvest with him.

~Based on Psalms 126:4-6

I thank You, Father, for teaching us that if You don't build our house, we labour in vain when we build it, and unless You watch over this city, the men who watch over it stand guard in vain. For we know that it is useless for us to work so hard from early morning until late night, anxiously toiling (working) for food to eat, when the Lord gives to His beloved children even in our sleep. Our children are a gift from the Lord; they are a reward from Him. Children born to a young man are like sharp arrows in the hands of a warrior. Happy is the man that has his patch full of them. He will not be put to shame when they confront their enemies at the city gates.

~Based on Psalms 127

I am blessed not to follow the advice of the wicked or hang out with sinners, or join in with them mocking others. I delight in doing everything the Lord wants from me. Day and night, I think about God's commands, laws and decrees, and know that I am like a tree planted by the waters bearing fruit each season without fail. My leaves will never wither, and I will prosper in all that I do.

~Based on Psalms 1:1-3

I give thanks to You, O Lord, and I proclaim Your greatness. I will let the whole world know what You have done. I will sing to You and tell everyone about Your miracles. I am Your chosen one. Thank You for standing by Your covenant You made with Abraham, the oath You swore to Isaac, and confirmed to Jacob as a decree. To Your people as a everlasting, never ending Treaty, You gave the land of Canaan as our special possession. Thank You for warning the devil not to touch Your chosen people, and to do Your prophets no harm. You are worthy of all praise! I give You all the glory praise and honor your deserve! Your faithfulness and Your Love endures forever.

~Based on Psalms 105:8-11

I will not let this book of God's Word depart out of my mouth. I shall meditate on the Word of God day and night. I will observe and do according to all that is written in it, for then God will make my way prosperous and I shall have good success.

~Based on Joshua 1:8

It doesn't make a difference whether people like or accept me because if God be for me, what man can be against me? He has given me grace and favor. God will shift the planet for me. If my ways please the Lord, He will make even my enemy be at peace with me. There is no one who can stop my destiny, but me. I stay in love at all times. My faith works by love and I trust God. The Church is the strongest institution in the world ever. I have diplomatic immunity because I represent the King of Kings and the Lord of Lords. Where ever I go, no evil shall befall me, nor shall any plague come near my dwelling. I trust and believe God's Word. I'm going to say what God says and do what God says to do. So let

God be true and every man be a liar. I declare and decree that the land You have given me is a pleasant land. What a wonderful inheritance!

~Based on Psalms 16:6

Lord, I know that the people who I love intended to harm me, but Lord, You intended it for my good to accomplish what is now being done: the saving of many lives. The Lord will bless me to provide for the ones I love and their children.

~Based on Genesis 50:20-21

Thank You, Father, for giving me the ability to produce wealth that You may establish Your covenant which You swore unto my forefathers, as it is this day.

~Based on Deuteronomy 8:18

So I take the word of God, and I am planting His word with my mouth into my heart. I will guard my ways night and day that I may not sin with my tongue. Whether I sleep or get up, the word sprouts and grows though I

don't know how. One plants, another waters, but God gives the increase and I have faith knowing that there is something happening on the inside of me. Though nothing now is showing, it is bringing forth my harvest.
~Based on Mark 4:26; Psalms 39:11; Mark 4:27

I'm so thankful Father that the sinner has a mission to gather flourishing cities, houses filled with good things, wells I did not dig, vineyards and olive groves I did not plant, and transfer it over to me.
~Based on Deuteronomy 6:10-11

I know how full of love and kindness You are Father, and though Jesus was very rich, yet for my sake He became poor so that by His poverty He has made me rich.
~Based on 2 Corinthians 8:9

Father, I Know You are able to make all grace abound for me, in all things, at all times, with my having all that I need. I will abound in every good work, and I have plenty left over to share with others.

~Based on 2 Corinthians 9:8

I waited patiently for the Lord to help me. He heard my cry, and He turned to me. He lifted me out of the pit of despair, out of the mud and the mire. He set my feet on solid ground and steadied me as He led me along. He has given me a new song to sing, a hymn of praise to my God. Many will see what He has done with me, and be astounded. They, too, will turn, and put their trust in the Lord. I take joy in doing Your will, my God, for Your law is written on my heart. I will not be afraid to speak out, as you well know. I have not kept this good news hidden. I have talked about Your faithfulness, Your saving power and Your unfailing love. May all who search and reach for You be filled with joy and gladness.

~Based on Psalms 40

Worthy is the lamb that was slain so I can receive my inheritance of power, riches, wisdom, strength, honor, glory and blessing.

The blessing will cause me to have favor and I'll get anything I request from God, He will turn things around for me in just days.

~Based on Revelation 5:11- 12

I will worship You, Father, in Your sanctuary and I ask that You allow me into Your presence. Help me to lead a blameless life and do what is right in Your eyes, speaking the truth with a sincere heart. Help me not to slander others, or harm neighbors or friends. I pray for the people that know that they are sinning, but keep doing it. I honor the people that follow after the Lord. I keep promises, even when it hurts. I lend money without interest and I don't accept bribes against the innocent. I am thankful to stand firm before You, Lord, forever and ever.

~Based on Psalms 15

I thank You, Father, for Your unfailing love to me and those who love You and obey Your commands. Listen to my prayer. I confess that we, Your people, have sinned against You by not obeying Your commands, laws and

decrees. We are Your chosen people who you rescue by Your mighty hand and power. Please forgive us Father for our sins.
~Based on Nehemiah 1:7

Father, You said only ask, so I'm asking. You said that You will give me the nations as my inheritance and the ends of the earth as my possession. You promised me if I ask, I will save the souls and get the property. No one can stop me from my inheritance, and by my speaking the Word I shall be justified. People are not my source, Father God; You are my only source and supply. Father, You promised that wealth and riches will be in my house, and I am so thankful for living a godly life.
~Based on Psalms 2:8; Galatians 1:12; Proverbs 8:18

I thank You, Holy Spirit, for teaching me what is best for me, and for directing me in the way I should go.
~Based on Isaiah 48:17

I thank You, Father God, that I am a King's Kid, and a King's Kid's command is backed by Your great power and no one can resist it or question it!

~Based on Ecclesiastes 8:4

I thank You, Father God, that I can come to You because I am thirsty… come to the waters without money. I come to buy and eat, buy wine and milk, without money and without a price. You fill me with wisdom and knowledge of Your will.

~Based on Isaiah 55:1

Father, come and stand beside me. Call me by my name. Speak to Your servant, for I am listening. I will let none of Your words fall to the ground. Appear to me and reveal Yourself to me through Your word.

~Based on 1 Samuel 3:10, 19, 21

There is no temptation taken me, except what is common to men: but God is faithful, who will not let me suffer by being tempted. My

Father will provide a way out that I can stand up and bear whatever it is.

~Based on 1 Corinthians 10:13

I Thank You, Father God, that Your divine power gives me everything I need for living a godly life. You have called me to receive Your own glory, and goodness. By that same mighty power, You have given me all of Your rich and wonderful promises. You have promised that I will escape the corruption all around me in this world caused by evil desires, and I am so thankful to You for it.

~Based on 2 Peter 1:3-4

I Thank You, Father, for putting Your words in my mouth and covering me with the shadow of Your hand, so that You may plant the heavens and lay the foundations of the earth, and say to the Church, "You are My people".

~Based on Isaiah 51:16-17

I do everything without complaining or arguing so that I may become a blameless and pure child of God without fault, in a crooked and depraved generation. I shine like a star in the universe, as I hold out the word of life, in order that I may boast on the day of Christ that I did not run or labor for nothing.

~Based on Philippians 2:14-16

I Thank You, Lord, that you have declared this day that I am your child, Your treasured possession, as You promised, and I will keep all Your commands. You have declared that You will set me in praises, fame, and honor, high above all nations that You have made, and that I am that child- holy to the Lord my God, as You promised.

~Based on Deuteronomy 26:18-19

(Insert your name), I am the Lord God, the holy one in Israel who teaches you, (insert your name), to profit and leadeth you, (insert your name), by the way you should go.

~Based on Isaiah 48:17

(Insert your name), I commit you to God, and the word of His grace, which is able to build you up, (insert your name), and give you an inheritance among all your brethren that are sanctified. You, (insert your name), shall decide and decree a thing so it shall be established for you. Where the word of a King is, (insert your name), there is power, and who can say what doest thou?

~Based on Acts 20:32

# SECTION TWO: PRAYING IN JESUS' NAME

I thank You, Father God, that I can do all things through Christ, Who gives me the strength, the will, and the ability. I thank You for the Blessing. I am willing to give my life for the word of God, and it will not return to Father God void. The blessing has changed every aspect of my life; it's so powerful to where I can start at one level, and go to a whole 'nother level. I do believe and embrace the blessing, the barakah. To have this blessing on my life that affects my finances gives me supernatural favor, supernatural promotion, prosperity, longevity, fruitfulness, protection, and business savvy to endure with power for success. It is a lifter, to lift me up and change my life, and I do not have to toil for it. I've been redeemed from groping; it will take me above all nations and all these blessings will overtake me and it will stick to me. People will be at awe of me. I am plentiful with goods and blessed with the work of my hands. I will lend to many nations, I shall not borrow. I shall be the head and not the tail. I shall be above only and not beneath. God has promoted me and is bringing me into leadership and the blessing has prospered me. God has chosen me and nobody can compete. I am saved. I am sanctified and I am filled with the Holy Ghost. If God be for me, there is not a man who can stand against me. God has sent me to fix it. God will through me bring it under kingdom jurisdiction. The blessing will pull down anything that comes against me. I believe God, I trust God, and I can take the devil down at any place. The blessings will protect me while I'm being raised up. People can dislike me all they want, but it will not make a difference. I just keep believing God and the blessing of Abraham will protect me, my family, our house, our cars, and our businesses. I do not walk by sight, I walk by faith. I wrestle not against flesh and blood but against principalities and powers of darkness, and I will stand and keep standing in Christ in Jesus' name. Amen.

Father, I ask You to forgive me of all my sins and iniquities. I don't ask You to forgive me because of the promises I've made, but because of Your Son Jesus who died on the Cross at Calvary for me. I repent, I surrender, I confess my sins to You, Father, and I thank You for my righteousness and the promises You made to me. I Love You, Lord, and I trust You in all things, especially your Vision for my life, in Jesus' name. Amen.

Father, You said in Your word that You will hear me when I call to You. Father, I'm going through this storm and I ask that You anoint this prayer that I pray for the people. I command that they all be healed completely of any kinds of afflictions, pain, crippling disorders, diseases, illnesses, handicaps, nervous system malfunctions, misfortunes, and sorrows. I cast all these sicknesses back into the pits of hell from which they come from, right now, in Jesus' name. I release healing and command that the people be restored to good health, from the top of their heads to the soles of their feet, by the blood of Jesus, in Jesus' name. Amen.

By the blood of Jesus, I pray against every evil force. I cast down every demonic force around me, my family and my home and I command it to leave us. In the name of Jesus I cast the demonic forces back into the pits of hell from which they come from, never to return, in Jesus' name. I'm releasing right now, right now the blood of Jesus on the blessings into our lives that the manifestation of what God has promised me in His word. I now expect it in our lives. I declare and decree it, in Jesus' name. Amen.

Father, I pray that all fathers be steady in whatever they do, in whatever they believe, and that they never compromise. I pray that fathers teach thier children about you, Father God, and how they should never waver in their trust in You. Let them always allow the word of God to be their foundation, and never let fear in their lives so they won't be scared to step out in faith on the things You tell them to do, and in seeking their desires. Father, a father should practice what he preaches, be constant and committed to what he says, believes and does, in Jesus' name. Amen.

Father God, I thank You for all You have done for me, for all You are doing for me, and for all You are going to do for me. You are the only One who I can depend on because You are my only source and supply. I place a demand on Your word, Father, and I ask that You grant me this prayer so my whole family and I can walk completely healed by the blood of Jesus. You said You will supply all our needs according to Your riches in glory by Christ Jesus, and I know Your word will not return to You void. You said in Your word to come boldly to Your throne of grace to obtain mercy and find grace to help in our time of need. I pray that my whole family is successful and filled with a deep and clear knowledge of Your word to bear fruit in every good work, in Jesus' name. I know that my righteous prayer is Your delight, as I delight myself in You. Thank You, Father, for providing my family with every possible avenue to ensure that we have a complete and total victory in this life, in Jesus' name. Amen.

Father, I ask for more knowledge. When You give a revelation, it's a revealed knowledge which is the main ingredient I need to build up my faith. I am so thankful that it opens my eyes to what says the Lord. It brings me freedom from every curse. When faith comes I will see it, then I'll start speaking it, and believing it. If I am harassed or even threatened, it will not stop me from saying what I believe, and then everything that is promised me or that I desire I'll receive. My faith will no longer be an option; it's a requirement. I thank You for this revelation, Father, in Jesus' name. Amen.

I thank You, Father God, that the windows of heaven are open for me and are enforcing the devil's defeat. I believe that I will experience things I've never seen. I thank You that Your dunamis power is mine, Your miracles are mine, and Your signs and wonders are all mine, in Jesus' name. Amen.

The love of God is so strong in me that I don't even think about fearing anything. I just want to get the job that He has called us to do done. I want to get His people out of poverty, out of jail, off drugs, and off the streets. I am an ambassador and representative for Christ. I thank You, Father, for choosing me and for blessing me with abundant grace and favor. I will not be timid or afraid because I know that You have placed me among wolves to bring the Kingdom of God to a dying world. I thank You for blessing them that bless me and cursing them that curse me. I thank You that the Holy Spirit which is in me will execute vengeance on those who stand in my way to stop me from fulfilling what You have called me to do in Jesus' name. Amen.

Father, You said in Your word that Your eyes move about on all the earth, to strengthen the heart that is completely toward You, and I am so thankful for Your strengthening my heart, in Jesus' name. Amen.

God said, "My people are destroyed for the lack of knowledge". Even though we have a new spirit, we now have to do something about our mind. Because our mind does not operate without a program and we have to reprogram our mind, so that it will be filled with the truth of God's Word. The Bible says cursed is a man who trusts in man, makes flesh his arm, and whose heart departs from God in Jesus' name. Amen.

Heavenly Father, I come to You in the name of Jesus to pray for the President of the United States of America and those in charge of our government. I pray that they hear You, Father God. I pray that they be surrounded by godly council. I pray that they make righteous decisions. I pray that they serve righteously before the people and not be prideful or arrogant in Jesus' name. Amen.

Father, this book of the law shall not depart out of my mouth, but I shall meditate on it day and night that I may observe to do according to all that is written in it. For it will then make my way prosperous and I shall have good success in Jesus' name. Amen.

Here I am, Lord. I'm here to do Your will, not my will, but Your will in my life. Holy Spirit, I'm everything with you, and nothing without you. I can't do God's will in my life without You. My heart is set to obey You, Father God, and to do what You have preplanned for me to do, today and always in Jesus' name. Amen.

I thank You, Father, for the Holy Spirit that He puts things in my heart to pray about. I thank You that He pleads my case before You. He is there to help me when I need help. He stays in close fellowship with me and teaches me spiritual things. He gives me spiritual recall when I am teaching or talking about You. I thank You for my spirit filled personality that is flooded with the anointing of You. I thank You that the more I obey You, the more I will do the good works You have preplanned for me to walk in and living the good life You have arranged for me to live. I give You my obedience, Father, and I thank You for this good life, in Jesus' name. Amen.

Father, I thank You for Your word. I thank You for the anointing that is on Your word. Father, I ask that You teach me how to make a heavenly withdrawal out of my heavenly treasure account, so that my every need will be meet each time I make a withdrawal, in Jesus' name. Amen.

O Lord God of Israel, there is no God like You in all heaven and earth. You keep Your promises and show Your unfailing love to all who obey You and are eager to do Your will. Father, You said in Your word that if the descendants of our forefathers will guard their hearts, behavior, and obey Your law, we will always reign. May You hear the humble and earnest requests from me, Your people, and when You hear us, please forgive us.

Teach us to do the right thing, and send rain on our land that You have given us as our special possession. Give us whatever we deserve, for You alone know our hearts. Then we will fear You and walk in Your ways as long as we live. If we sin, we will turn back to You with our whole hearts. Forgive us who have sinned. Father, I ask that You be attentive to all of our prayers, and do not reject Your anointed. Remember Your unfailing love for Your servant this day, in Jesus' name. Amen.

Father, I know that You have plans for me of hope and a future. The devil will not derail me in any way because You lead and guide me, and I'm so thankful to You for it, in Jesus' name. Amen.

I thank you, Father, that with me being a joint heir with Christ, who owns all things, I ask that You give me the spirit of wisdom, and revelation in the knowledge of You, in Jesus' name. Amen.

Father, remove any hurt; cleanse away evil, as Your stripes heal the inner depths of my heart. Father, I ask that You sit me down and teach me. Lord, lift me up and bless me to speak forth Your word in truth to anyone as You lead me, in Jesus' name. Amen.

By the blood of Jesus, I command the devil to take his hands off my family. I command the spirits that are operating around my family that are negative to be neutralized right now, in Jesus' name. I cast the devil out of our homes, our cars, our jobs, our businesses and cast that devil back to the pits of hell where he came from. I release the abundance of joy, love, peace, and being productive in all that we do, in Jesus' name. Amen.

I declare that I have God's own faith within me. I have the same measure of faith that Jesus Himself has. What I speak out of my mouth and believe in my heart will come to pass. I stay in faith by refusing to fear and by giving thanks to God, in Jesus' name. Amen.

Father, I ask You to give me an unlimited imagination with dreams and visions to have and achieve the impossible. You said in Your word that if I hold fast to what I believe as I meditate on the word of God that what I see I will achieve, in Jesus' name. Amen.

Father, You have blessed me with a long and satisfying life. You have brought me out of the darkness into this awesome light. You supply all my needs according to Your riches and glory. I ask You to bless and heal my family. I thank You that I have food in my house, and all my debts are paid. I am blessed with good health and strength, and I thank You for blessing me with an abundance of wealth and power. I give You all the glory, praise and honor for it, in Jesus' name. Amen.

Father, give me a hearing heart, a wise and understanding heart, and a generous heart of wisdom, in Jesus' name. Amen.

Thank You, Father God, for showing me in Your word the steps I need to take to get the results You want in my life, in Jesus' name. Amen.

I thank You, Father, that You didn't ask me to pay for it. You asked me to believe for it, in Jesus' name. Amen.

Father, I ask for divine connections with the right people in my life. I ask that You give me wisdom and insight so that I can see the root of whatever is going on in my life. I ask for Your guidance to do Your will in my life. I put all my trust in You, Father God, because You saved my life. Lord, do me a favor. Every morning, in the name of Jesus, I declare favor over my life. I expect favor and a shield of faith to surround me, and doors to open for me that no man can close. No hindrance can stop me. I am the apple of Your eye. I am blessed and highly favored before God. Breaking into new levels of favor as I reign as king, I walk in the power and authority of God. As I rise to the top of high places with divine favor, restoration, and confidence, God will open any door and laws will change.

Where God lifts me up, the battle has already been won, and I don't have to fight. One encounter with God is worth a lifetime of labor, and I walk in it, in Jesus name. Amen.

I thank You, Father God, that I am generous because of my faith. I am praying that You will really put my generosity to work, for in doing so, I will come to an understanding of all the good things I can do for Christ, in Jesus' name. Amen.

I am the seed of Abraham through Jesus Christ, and Father, You said in Your Word that You will make me a great nation, and will bless me and make my name great. I will be a blessing, dispensing goods to others, in Jesus' name. Amen.

May God always give me plenty of dew for healthy crops and good harvests of grain and wine, in Jesus' name. Amen.

I believe my future is in my heart. It doesn't matter how many people are against me who don't want me to succeed. No one can stop me from getting property, or becoming a billionaire! No person, no government, no terrorist organization, no one. It doesn't make a difference who they are, what they believe, or how big they come. I know God has given me this promise that out of the abundance of my heart, my mouth speaks, and a good man out of a good deposit is going to bring forth good things. I declare and decree it, in Jesus' name. Amen.

Whatever God is going to put in my hands has to first be spoken out of my mouth, in Jesus' name. Amen.

Thank You, Father, for extending Your favor in order to advance Your kingdom. I am blessed to accomplish Your will and Your purpose in my life, in Jesus' name. Amen.

I am what the Bible says I am. I can do what the scripture says I can do. I don't care about hostile forces trying to make me go back into my own ability. I am anointed by the

Anointed One. The Holy Ghost is in me now giving me what only God can do. My days of struggle are over. From this day forward, I shall have sweatless victories in my life, in Jesus' name. Amen.

I am what the Bible says I am. I can do what the scripture says that I can do which is all things through Christ, the Anointed One, and His anointing that strengthens me. God said I am royalty so I believe it, I receive it, and I'm walking in it from this day forward. The devil will bow because he is under my feet. I am God's child and He is the King of Kings. Anything that is not of God shall not go on in my life. My days of getting frustrated, shouting, yelling, getting evil, talking about people, and gossiping are over. I am not just a King's Kid, I am Royalty. I am like a Queen Esther; I've been chosen for such a time as this. Now it's time to work in Jesus' name. Amen.

I have the blessing of Abraham on me, in me, through me, and I am wealthy. With this blessing on my life, I draw resources. I am a money magnet. I draw money. I draw contracts. I draw wealth. The Lord will command the blessings on my storehouse, in all I set my hands to, and He will bless me in the land which the Lord my God has given me in Jesus' name. Amen.

Father God, I thank You that You have set before me life and death; blessings and cursing; so I choose life that my children and I may live. I love You, God, and obey Your voice. I cling to You because You are my life and the length of my days. I will live in the land You swore to my forefathers for me. Father, I come boldly to Your throne of grace to obtain favor and find grace to help in my time of need. Be merciful to me, and cause Your face to shine on me that Your ways may be known on the earth. I ask for favor with my whole heart knowing I am not worthy to be called a minister or an evangelist, but by Your grace I am what I am, and it's not in vain. I will do Your will, not my will, but

Your will be done in my life, in Jesus' name. Amen.

The job of the Holy Spirit is to deal with any one who comes to make me uncomfortable. By staying in the full purpose of God, I'm going to fulfill my destiny; there have been strongholds that have been delaying me. I should be owning my own building, owning my own business, but there has been spiritual resistance that has been working against me. Whatever has been coming against me, this is the last day. My God has given me the knowledge I need to know that even if I go into the worst situation, the devil cannot touch me. I am the apple of God's eye. God says, "Touch not my anointed and do my prophets no harm" and "No weapon formed against me shall prosper, and every tongue that rises against me shall be condemned". God will make me a great nation, make my name great and I will be a blessing by dispensing goods to others. My God will bless them that bless me, and curse them that curse me. Whatever my destiny, I will fulfill my destiny. Nothing is going to harm me. The Holy Spirit's main job is to execute vengeance upon all my enemies, the enemies of God's people. Thank You, Holy Spirit, for guarding me, and my angels for watching over me. I'm not concerned about hurt, harm, accidents or danger because my God is going to take care of every one of them, in Jesus' name. Amen.

Father, every time I try to correct something that is wrong in my life, it gets worse. Yet, when I get out of Your way by casting my cares on You, and letting You handle it, I become a conqueror in all things. I just let go and let God, in Jesus' name. Amen.

Father, You promised me in Your word that if I obey and serve You that I will spend my days in prosperity, and my years in pleasures, in Jesus' name. Amen.

I decree the truth is that I am wealthy. I decree that I am not here to take sides with different religions, but to do what God says. I decree that by His stripes, I am healed. I decree that I can lay hands on the sick and they shall recover, in Jesus' name. Amen.

I decree from this day forward that I will win every battle which comes against my mind, and do so speedily, in Jesus' name. Amen.

I thank You, Father, that I am not carnally minded, but I'm spiritually minded with abundance of wealth and power, a lot of love, a long life, and a peace that surpasses all understanding. I declare and decree it, in Jesus' name. Amen.

I thank You, Father, for the power that you released in my life. There is no real advancement without this principal requirement of power that is on me to reverse anything that the devil has done, in Jesus' name. Amen.

I have received Jesus into my heart, and I have been engrafted into Gods royal family. I am a King's Kid; that is the revelation of my royalty. I am a speaking spirit, and everything in the universe must adjust itself to the words I speak. The Church is the most powerful institution on this earth ever. I will rise higher with the words I speak. There is a King in me, and I understand my divinity. My thinking is elevated above how I used to think. I will advance God's kingdom, I will transform myself so God can transform this world through me. I declare and decree it, in Jesus' name. Amen.

Father, though the fig tree may not blossom, nor fruit be on the vine, I still rejoice in You. I have dreams and goals for which I am still believing. There are situations I'm praying will turn around. Father, I know that there's always a period of waiting involved from the time I pray until the time it comes to pass. During these trials of faith are when many people get discouraged and give up. They start believing negative thoughts, but not me! My prayers still have potential, but I have to do my part. I must start watering my seed (my prayers) and I do that by thanking You, Father, in advance, and declaring Your word.

I will not wait until I receive it to thank You, Father, because I'm praising You and thanking You that it's on its way, in Jesus' name. Amen.

I thank You, Father, that I have a blood covenant with You. You are my Heavenly Father, and You are rich and powerful. I thank You for backing me as surely as You backed Abraham, and as surely as You backed Jesus Himself. That makes me blessed with every spiritual blessing in heavenly places, and I am the righteousness of God by Christ. The blessings of Abraham are surely mine, in Jesus' name. Amen.

In the midst of a famine God gives me double the money, double the food, and double the provision, in Jesus' name. Amen.

Father God, I thank You for filling me with Your spirit, with skills, abilities and being knowledgeable of all kinds of crafts, designs and work, in Jesus' name. Amen.

I declare and decree that no matter what I'm facing, I know God is greater than all of it. I don't believe the lies of the devil. I keep being faithful to God, and I honor God in all that I do. I thank God that He is in control over me. I thank God for fighting my battles. I thank God that new doors are opening for me. I thank God that no weapons formed against me will prosper, and I am content because my harvest is here, in Jesus' name. Amen.

There is nothing too hard for God. With God all things are possible. I may be up against a Red Sea, but I just stretch out my hands, and I speak the word of God. Many afflictions may try and come on me but my God will deliver me from them all. I can draw water out of the well of salvation, but one word from God can change my life forever, in Jesus' name. Amen.

I thank You, Father, that I am in the kingdom, and I get exactly what I expect. I expect favor from You, Father God, in these last days. I expect new doors to be opened for me. I expect policies to be changed for me. I expect privileged treatment like Queen Esther. I expect You, Father, to fight battles that I don't have to fight. I expect someone to recognize who I am and give me a high position for no reason at all. I expect honor in the midst of my adversaries. I expect restoration of everything that the devil has stolen from me. I am entitled to divine favor as a covenant child of the Living God, in Jesus' name. Amen.

I am envied, not pitied. I have the blessing of Abraham on me, in me, and through me, and I am wealthy. I am blessed going in, blessed coming out, and all my debts are canceled — God says so, in Jesus' name. Amen.

Father God, I ask You to always bring all things to my remembrance and whatsoever You have said to me, in Jesus' name. Amen.

Father, I pray that You open the eyes of my understanding, and command me to be blessed with all spiritual blessings in heavenly places, so all the blessings are mine throughout eternity and even before the foundation of the world. Oh, Father God, fill my spirit with light and understanding about what You did for me through Jesus on the cross, and His power towards me through the resurrection. Thank You, Lord, in Jesus' name. Amen.

Father, I thank You for calling me to be a fellow workman, a laborer together with You. I submit myself to Your leadership, and I thank the Holy Spirit for interceding for me. Thank You for loving me so much that You choose me to be Your representative to spread the gospel of Jesus Christ all over the world.

Father, I ask that the gospel of Jesus always be first in my life, knowing and believing that Jesus died on the cross at Calvary for me. Father, I believe that You created the world, the stars, the moon, yes, even man, at no cost. But when You sacrificed Your only Son to save if not but just one man, You gave everything. Thank You for Your Son Jesus, and the blood that He shed for me, my family, and the world. Thank You for picking me to represent You, to teach what Jesus did for us all over the world, in Jesus' name. Amen.

I thank You, Father that there is no more lack in my house. If I have something I need in my house, all I have to do is sow a seed into the Kingdom of God, in Jesus' name. Amen.

Father, I know You have plans for me, and You have put me in a place so I will obey and follow You. I don't need to pay attention to what it looks like, I'll just go on and do what You said to do because You have a plan for me, and my provision is a part of that plan. I won't pay any attention to what the world has or doesn't have for me. I'll just let You take care of them, and take care of me, in Jesus' name. Amen.

Lord command Your light to shine on me, and give me a revelation that reveals to me what I can't see, and what I don't know, in Jesus' name. Amen.

I give all my Praise to You, Lord. You are my salvation. You are my deliverer. You are my healer. You are my provider. You are my Protector. You are my Peace. You are my Joy. You are my all and all. I'm going to praise You in the morning. I'm going to praise You at night. I'm going to praise You when I'm up and I'm going to Praise You when I'm down, in Jesus' name. Amen.

I thank You, Father that I am an overcomer! I overcome weakness with strength. I overcome falsehood with truth. I overcome evil with good. I overcome anxiety with peace. I overcome fear with faith. I overcome confusion with wisdom. I overcome temptation with scripture, and everything with Praise, in Jesus' name. Amen.

I thank You, Father God, that everything I need You have already done for me. Thank You for blessing me with what I didn't even know to ask You for, in Jesus' name. Amen.

I thank You, Father, for Jesus, and for Him redeeming us from the curse of the law. I thank You, Father, for giving me keys of authority to whatever I bind, forbid, and declare to be improper, and unlawful on earth is already bound in heaven. Whatever I loose, permit, and declare lawful on earth is already loosed in heaven. I am thankful for You building me up as a King's Kid. Your mature offspring are to receive revelation from You. Thank You for calling us to take back control, and bring things in line with the Kingdom of God. We are here to finish what Adam started, to plant the garden of Eden throughout the earth. I've been delivered out of darkness, fear, and worry. I have success in all things because the Holy Spirit dwells inside me. Allow me to picture Your thoughts because Your anointing is flowing in and through me, in Jesus' name. Amen.

Father God, I know that we should always tithe because when we don't, it seems like we have a bag of money with holes in it. I believe we should give, and sow seed, especially when I am in financial trouble. Father, I believe that when You tell me to do something, I should obey You and do it right then because You are trying to get something to me. I pray for the President and all the leaders of the government—on all levels. I pray that I always tell the truth, and for me to remember that there is no such thing as a little white lie, and to never say I can't afford it. Father, I want to always keep my word even to my own hurt. I pray that I don't allow strife to exist in my life. I pray that I do what is right because it's right, and then do it right then even if no one is looking. I believe that parents should not spare the rod. I believe that he who spares the rod hates his son, but he who loves him is careful to discipline him. I pray to love all people, and to let them live their lives. I believe it is not right to judge others nor is it my place to correct others, in Jesus' name. Amen.

I thank You, Father, for providing me with a permanent home land, a secure place where I will never be disturbed. It is mine where wicked people won't oppress me. I thank You for subduing all my enemies. Who am I, Father God, and who is my family that You have brought us this far? You know who and what I am, and according to Your will You have done all these great things for me, and have made them known. Father, there is no other God like You. How many other people have You brought out of the darkness into this marvelous light? You have performed awesome miracles and drove away people who stood in my way. May the dynasty of Your servant be established in Your presence. You are my God, O Lord. You have blessed me and my family so that our dynasty will continue forever before You. I pray that you make it eternal, in Jesus' name. Amen.

I keep my body under subjection and I tell my body that it is healed. I am a speaking spirit, and the body profits nothing. I have divine nature in me to function just like God, so I speak to my body and command my body to be healed, in Jesus' name. I can speak things, and everything in the universe must adjust itself to the words I speak. I am completely healed by the stripes of the Lord Jesus Christ from the top of my head to the soles of my feet, by the blood of Jesus, in Jesus' name. Amen.

The memory of the righteous is blessed, and I thank You, Father God, for bringing all things to my remembrance. I thank You that everything You sat me down to teach me will flow out of me like rivers of living water, in Jesus' name. Amen.

I do not cease to pray and make special requests of You Father God, asking that You fill me with the deep and clear knowledge of Your will, all spiritual wisdom, and purposes of You in understanding and discernment of spiritual things, in Jesus' name. Amen.

Father, I pray that the eyes of my understanding will be enlightened that I will know what is the hope of Your calling for me. Anything that you have provided for me that has been stolen by the devil, may my eyes see it and my faith will take it back. I pray in Jesus' name that anything that has been stolen from me is on its way back to me speedily, in Jesus' name. Amen.

I am the daughter of the most High God, a King's Kid. By my being His child, I am an heir also…an heir with God and fellow heir with Christ Jesus, sharing His inheritance with Them. As long as I am a child then I am heir over the whole estate, in Jesus' name. Amen.

I thank You, Father God, that I have a kingdom mindset. You said in your word that sound wisdom is better than weapons of war. So I thank You, Father God, that I have the wisdom to rise and dispossess squatters and dismantle systems. I thank You that with my kingdom mindset, I can see things different, and can get the revelation of things that other people can't get. Because the mysteries of the kingdom of God are being revealed to me as I line up with the kingdom thinking, it is so, in Jesus' name. Amen.

Father, save me from the clenches of the powerful so that at least I have hope, and the fangs of the wicked are broken against me, in Jesus' name. Amen.

Father, I know where You are taking me is impossible, but I receive it. That is why I have faith, because my faith connects me to You, Father God, and with You Father, all things are possible. Wherever I see the impossible in my life, that's where my stuff is that's possible and I'm going to get it, in Jesus' name. Amen.

I thank You, God that I was born so that Jesus could be revealed through me, in Jesus' name. Amen.

Father, I pray that the eyes of my understanding be flooded with light, where I can see things that some people can't see. If I can see things some people can't see then I can have things some people can't have. I can go places that some people can't go. I can do things that some people can't do. I'm Your child, Father God. You are taking me to the top and causing me to be in leadership, in Jesus' name. Amen.

God is not fair, but He is just. I thank You, Father, that You give me the ability to use my potential to explode in this earth. This ability to create allows me to go as far as I can, and be as much as I can be. I know once I sow my seed into the Kingdom of God, that You, Father take it, and multiply it so I won't be limited. I can live on my potential. I thank You for opening within me business ideas, and giving me the power to get wealth, being able to override the curse of the earth. Thank You for blessing me regardless of what is going in the economy, in Jesus' name. Amen.

# SECTION 3: SPECIFIC PRAYERS

How God Sees Me

I thank You, Father, for seeing me as a King's kid, as a joint heir with Jesus Christ, and as a child of the Most High God. I thank You that I am seated with Jesus in heavenly places. I am the righteousness of God through Christ Jesus. I am a ruler. I'm an ambassador. I'm an offspring. I'm superior. I am wealthy, in charge and a leader in Jesus' name. Amen.

He That Dwells in the Secret Place

God alone is my refuge, my place of safety; in Him will I trust. He will rescue me from every trap, and protect me from the plague. He will cover me with His wings, and I will find refuge. His promises are faithful, and is my armor and protection. I will not fear the terror of the night, nor fear the dangers of the day, nor the plague that walks in darkness. Though a thousand fall at my side, and ten thousand are dying at my right hand, these evils will not come near me because I will see it with my eyes to see how the wicked are punished. Because I have made the Lord my dwelling place, and my shelter, no evil will conquer me. He commands His angels to protect me wherever I go. They will lift me up with their hands to keep me from striking my foot against a stone. I will crush fierce lions, and serpents under my feet. God loves me, and He will protect me because I acknowledge His name. I will call on the Lord, and He will answer. He will be with me in times of trouble. He will rescue me and give me honor. With long life will He satisfy me, and give me His salvation, in Jesus' name. Amen.

~Based on Psalms 91:1-16

I Am God Almighty

Walk before me and be blameless. I will confirm my covenant between Me and you and will greatly increase your numbers. I will make you very fruitful; I will make nations of you, and Kings will come from you. I will establish my covenant as an everlasting covenant between Me, you, and your descendants after you for generations to come to be your God. I will give the Promised Land as an everlasting possession to you and your descendants after you, and I will be their God. As for you, you must keep my covenant…you and your descendants after you for generations to come. The covenant you are to keep is: every male among you shall be circumcised, and it will be the sign of the covenant between Me and you. My covenant in your flesh is to be an everlasting covenant, in Jesus' name. Amen.

~Based on Genesis 17:1-14

Prophecy for the Church

I thank You, Father, for telling us to not remember the former things, to not consider the things of old. You want us to know that You are doing a new thing! Now it springs forth. You want to know if we perceive it, know it, and if we give heed to it! You will even make a way in the wilderness and rivers in the desert for us. Thank You, Father, for helping, operating, saving, and advancing our lives in new ways. Thank You for telling us that we are in a new season, and that You have ordained us to go forward, in Jesus' name. Amen.

~Based on Isaiah 43:18-19

## Family and Friends Prayer

Heavenly Father, I ask You to grant me this prayer for my family and friends. I command them to come up out of the mindset of complaining about everything and being negative. They shall not be easily stressed out because things don't go the way they planned for them to go. I command them to know that they are not limited. I command them to think big, and for them to know that it's a choice to being happy. I command them to know it's time to come out of their comfort zone. They should allow themselves to experience a different way of living, a way that they are more than worthy of having. I command that they step out to know you, God, because once they know You, the devil's ability to deceive them into complaining, being negative, or stressing out will go away. It's the devil's plan to keep them stuck, fearful, and not want to move forward. I command them to have hope, dreams, plans and desires for their future. I command for them to know that they deserve to be happy, to have love, joy, peace, and for them to know that they can have that with You, Father, in Jesus' name. Amen.

## The Blessing of Abraham

I thank You, Father, that the blessing of Abraham has come on me, (insert your name), that I have receive the promise of the Spirit through faith. You said wherever I go to expect to be blessed going in and blessed going out. I expect people who don't even like me to give me grace and favor. I expect by faith to come up with business strategies, and everything I lay my hands on by faith will come forth. By faith, I have sound wisdom to solve business strategies and business problems, in Jesus' name. Amen.

## A Prayer for the Pastor

Heavenly Father, I come to You in the name of my Lord and Savior Jesus Christ, on behalf on Your child, Pastor (insert pastor's name here). I thank You, Father God, that he/she is a true leader and that he/she points us in the ways of You to do Your will. I thank You, Father God, that he/she is a King's kid, and You allow him/her to have more than enough to do for Your people. For You said in Your word that You will open the windows of heaven and pour out such a blessing that there will not be room enough to receive it all. I thank you for rebuking the devourer for his/her sake, and his/her heart will be filled with thanksgiving. I thank You, Father, that he/she is the head and not the tail, and that he/she is always in Your presence. I pray that he/she seeks first Your kingdom and Your righteousness. I pray that he/she is continually led by the Holy Spirit. I ask that no evil befall him/her and that he/she stays surrounded and encamped by the Holy Spirit and His angels at all times. Give him/her wisdom in everything that he/she says or does. Keep him/her in perfect health, joy, and peace. Let every good prophecy that has been spoken into his/her life come to pass. I bind any curse that has been placed on his/her life, and I command the devil to keep his hands off him/her, in Jesus' name. I loose the blessings of the Lord to overtake him/her and I thank You, Father, that he/she gives to the needy and works on behalf of the poor. I ask you, Father, to extend Your blessings to him/her in Your name, that Your Name will be praised forever, in Jesus' mighty name. Amen.

A Prayer for the Pastor and Congregation
I thank You, Father, for Pastor <u>(insert the pastor's name here)</u> and for him/her being committed to Your will and Your work. I ask that You bless them and their family. I ask that he/she stays in good health and strength. Grant wisdom in everything he/she says or does. I thank You for the classes that the pastor teaches the congregation about You. I thank You for the spiritual warriors who cover him/her in prayer. I ask that You pour out Your blessings and favor on their lives. I ask You to bless the other ministers who serve with the pastor and keep them in the palm of Your hand. I pray for the congregation that they come to know Jesus, and what a great sacrifice He gave on the cross for us. I pray

that we all pay our tithes and offerings with a thankful heart having faith in You, Father, as we should, and be healed of all sin, sickness, and disease, in Jesus' name. Amen.

A Prayer for Daughters and Granddaughters
Father, I ask that You turn every curse sent my daughter and granddaughter's way into a blessing. Help them to be disciplined enough to obey You, so they can become the persons You created them to be. Father, I ask that You put a watch over their mouths, and keep their tongues from evil. Help them to put all their expectations in You, Father, and not in this world or its system so that they can grow into a life that is godly, exciting, and spiritually productive, in Jesus' name. Amen.

A Prayer for Travel
(dedicated to Auna and Kevin)
Father, I ask that Your powerful arm guide and protect (Insert loved one's names) for a safe trip. I trust You, Father, to watch over them to keep them safe. Let Your hand cover them at night until the dawn of each day. I

pray that the engineer be a safe driver and that they have a great crew. Let them have a peaceful, restful and relaxing trip. I ask that they have grace and favor with everyone they encounter. I pray that they return home and find it better than they left it, with the children healthy, strong, and happy in Jesus' name. Amen.

A Prayer Against Accidents or Incidents
Father, in the name of Jesus, I lift up (insert name) and (insert name) to You. I pray that you put a hedge of protection around them. I thank You, Father, that they choose life, and they obey Your voice. I ask You Father to give them grace and favor with everyone that they encounter on this trip, and that You bless them and cause Your face to shine on them. Let no accident overtake them nor plague, calamity, or road rage come near them. I ask that You give Your angels charge over them so not a hair on their head will perish. I thank You, Father God, in advance for their safe trip to their destination and back home, in Jesus' name. Amen.

A Prayer for My Daughter's Wedding

Father, in the name of Jesus, I pray that (insert name of bride) and (insert name of groom) put their trust in You. I pray that they lean on You, rely on You, have confidence in You, knowing that You will always be there for them. I pray that they are entering into a healthy relationship, one in which both of them will grow together spiritually and in love. I pray that they delight in each other, be of the same mind and spirit, and that their prayers be not hindered in any way. I pray that they seek You first and Your Kingdom and righteousness so that all things will be added to them. I pray that they enter into a healthy marriage with You being the head over their lives. I pray that they delight in each other as they delight in You, and for You to give them the desires of their hearts, united in the Spirit of You. Father, I pray that You teach them how not to have their prayers hindered in any way, and for them to express themselves in marriage being honorable unto You, in Jesus' name. Amen.

## A Graduation Prayer

Father, I thank You for (insert name of graduate) and for bringing them to this milestone in their life. Graduation is such an important time and now their life will give way to twists and turns to help the future unfold. I pray that they will apply all that has been learned up until now, and that You, Father, will teach them Your ways, and guide them along the path that You would have them to go. Give them wisdom in the choices that they will have to make, and I pray that they will have sound judgment in the challenges that lie ahead. I pray that they have lots of love, integrity and grace, and that it will manifest itself in the direction that they choose to go. Make them steady in faith and may they put all their trust in You, Father, especially when the trials and tribulations come which cause some people go astray. I pray that You guide them socially, financially and spiritually in all things, and I pray that as they are coming into adulthood, they will keep You, Father, as the Rock upon which they will be grounded, in Jesus' name. Amen.

## A Prayer for a Godly Life

But you, (insert name), belong to God; so run from all these evil thoughts and things, and follow what is right and good. Pursue a godly life along with trusting God, with faith, love, perseverance, and gentleness in spite of difficulty. Fight the good fight for what you believe. Hold tightly to eternal life that God has given you (insert name), which you (insert name) have confessed so well before many witnesses. I command you (insert name) before God, who gives life to all, and before Jesus Christ, who gave a good testimony before Pilate, that you (insert name) obey His commands with all purity. May no one can find fault with you (insert name) from now until our Lord Jesus Christ returns, in Jesus' name. Amen.

A Prayer for the Backslider
(Dedicated to Andrew)

Heavenly Father, I come to You in the name of my Lord and Savior Jesus Christ. I ask You, Father God, to show me the path where I should walk and to point out the right road for me to follow. Lead me by Your truth, and teach me for You are the God who saves me. All day long, I put my hope in You. Remember O Lord, Your unfailing love and compassion which You have shown from long past. Forgive the rebellious sins of my past. Look instead through the eyes of Your unfailing love and be merciful to me. You are my God, O Lord, and You do what is right. You show the proper path to those who go astray, and You lead the humble in what is right, teaching them Your way. Turn to me and have mercy on me for I am alone and in deep distress. My problems go from bad to worse. Father, I ask that You save me from all of them. Feel my pain, see my trouble and forgive me of all my sins. Protect me; rescue my life. Do not let me be disgraced, for I trust in You. For I put my hope in You. Father, ransom me (insert your name) from my troubles, in Jesus' name. Amen.

~Based on Psalms 25:4-9; 16-22

### A Prayer For Your City

Father, I pray for (insert name of your city). I Thank You, Father, that I am a visionary leader and in You, I can see the current circumstances of (insert name of your city), and how I can lead this city and nation safety into its destiny. With You, Father, causing me to rise up as a modern-day Joseph, (insert name of your city) and every city like it, can be transformed to become the economic envy of the world. I declare and decree that I'm being raised up as a visionary leader for this time right now, in Jesus' name. Amen.

ABOUT THE AUTHOR

As a former home care provider, tending to the needs of others is ingrained in the DNA of first-time author, Evangelist Charity Turner. Gifted to nurture, Evangelist Turner goes above and beyond for people – be it family or strangers. She has exercised her gift throughout her career through acts of servitude in community organizations. Evangelist Turner has worked with the homeless community as the former manager of Serving People in Need (S.P.I.N.), along with her own initiative, King Kids International LLC.